# UILDER BOARDS

How to construct a set of
notched boards children use to
create their own play space

## Jack McKee

**HANDS ON BOOKS**

1117 Lenora Court

Bellingham, WA 98225

(360) 671-9079

ISBN 1-884894-52-6
Cover photo by David Scherrer
Text photos by Candy Meacham, Jack McKee

# ACKNOWLEDGEMENTS

## BUILDER BOARDS

Many people helped and encouraged me throughout the design, building, and writing about Builder Boards. I'd like to thank them all. Kathie and Steve Wilson of the Childlife Montessori School for trusting me with their students despite my lack of formal training. Carl Chamberlin for the five-notch idea. Debbie Todd-Stone for the drawings. Paddy Bruce for the cover design and page layout. Robin Crookall and Griffin Hunt for permission to use their drawings. Jamie Todd-Stone and Annika Stoner for this cover photo. Candy Meacham for help with writing and for putting up with all my strange ideas over the years. Paul Cocke for the editing. A special thanks to the kids whose smiles, laughter and enthusiasm kept me building and motivated me to write.

## EIGHTH GRADE PROJECT

My thanks to all those involved with the eighth grade project. Julee Pitalo at Whatcom Middle School in Bellingham for saying, "When can we start?" Whatcom Middle School and Western Washington University's Campus Compact for sponsoring the project. Terry Pickeral and Emi Fredlund for their help and encouragement. Carolee Cummings and Steve Freuhling, Washington Serve volunteers, for their able assistance supervising the kids. Rory Fanning, Sharon Hippi and Tom Chamberlin for their video editing expertise. Most of all, thanks to the kids who built the set: Cory Graves, Tanner Stone, Ben Varco-Merth, Nicky Lee, Jon Hornberger, Nichole Allen, Khai Huynh, Frank Buckner and Abram Bergstrom.

# CONTENTS

# INTRODUCTION

As any parent can attest, children learn by doing. As their mentors, adults need to provide children with opportunities to use their eyes, hands and imaginations to order their own environments, to control their own child-sized worlds.

Builder Boards, a set of notched boards, inspires children to do just that by acting as building blocks of a child's imagination—allowing her to inhabit an idea with her hands and mind. A child's imagined playhouse, fort, cabin or cave can be assembled, modified, built and rebuilt into reality.

Builder Boards allow children to make decisions and to solve problems, both independently and as a group. They learn how to plan ahead, to visualize something taking shape and then to take action on their planning. The end result gives them a sense of accomplishment—of something they organized and developed from beginning to end.

Builder Boards began as a playhouse for the children of the Montessori school where I worked. Building for kids has always been very satisfying for me because children are by nature appreciative and are impressed by handmade items. I knew how much my own children enjoyed building and how much they liked their own small space.

*Kindergartners showing off their creation.*

As I watched the preschoolers build with blocks, I began thinking of a playhouse they could actually build themselves. I experimented with materials, rejecting real logs as too heavy, cardboard tubes and plastic plumbing pipe as too awkward. I then decided on cedar fence boards: they are light, locally available and look like a mini-log cabin.

*Older children build more complicated structures.*

Initial tests with neighborhood kids were successful so I took the pieces for a complete play-house to my preschool class at the Montessori school and asked, "Who wants to help build a play-house?" Naturally, everyone did. Chaos ensued. Kids bumped into each other, walked on boards and there was confusion about which board to put on next. It didn't take long to realize that eight preschoolers were too many for one playhouse. But once we got down to three or four kids at a time they were able to proceed.

Eventually, they got the walls up and were ready for the roof. Yet in my excitement to test the playhouse, I hadn't built the roof yet. The neighborhood kids had seemed satisfied with a blanket, so I brought out a blanket for the preschoolers. Big disappointment. I had to promise to bring the "real roof" the next week. I did build a roof to complete the set. The kids approved of this finishing touch, and plans for this cedar playhouse are in the first chapter.

Although I was pleased by my creation, during the next two years, children taught me that it could be much more than a playhouse. Using their imaginations, they hardly ever built the standard playhouse, instead building a house with two doors and windows everywhere and a house with no doors or windows at all. Once they built a house with a tunnel entrance and a flat roof. After that came caves, castles, forts, towers and a hot dog stand. The idea of building just a playhouse gave way to the idea of building from a child's imagination. The result was Builder Boards.

From watching children use the playhouse, I learned intermediate-sized pieces would allow more options. I redesigned the long wall piece to have five equally spaced notches and five different length wall pieces: each with two, four, six, eight or ten notches. Preschoolers are more comfortable with fewer notches; older kids, because they often make more elaborate structures, tend to prefer more notches.

*Pre-schoolers are more comfortable with short boards.*

I chose plywood as the building material for this new set, since plywood made the set practically indestructible and eliminated the need for a planer during construction. Plans for this plywood set are in the second chapter.

Since then, Builder Boards has undergone rigorous use in classrooms, at a summer camp for disabled children and as a part of a traveling science program, and always attracted a crowd of eager young builders. Teachers and parents seemed to like them as much as the kids.

Builder Boards was developing a life of its own and, just when I thought I was finished, the kids showed me another step.

At a children's fair, some middle school students came by and wanted to try to build a playhouse. Not only were they eager to use Builder Boards, but they wanted to build a set themselves. I was surprised and then intrigued. Reflecting, I realized that with jigs, kids could build a set even without much woodworking experience. Several possibilities came to mind:

- Fourth or fifth graders could build a set for their own school with parents building the jigs and supervising
- A high school student could do the project from beginning to end as a senior project or as community service
- A Girl or Boy Scout could construct a set of Builder Boards as a combined community service–carpentry merit badge

Kids working on such a project would learn about the importance of careful work, persistence, practical math, organization and planning. Best of all, it would plant the idea of building for others–a mini-Habitat for Humanity in action.

Taken with the idea, I started proposing it to anyone who would listen: teachers, PTA members and scout leaders. I was contacted by a local middle school teacher who asked me to supervise eighth graders constructing a set of Builder Boards as part of their service learning project.

The fourth chapter documents this service learning project in which nine 8th graders measured, cut, notched, beveled, sanded, oiled, stapled, glued and videotaped the construction process. After serious deliberation, which was an important part of the process, they choose the Bellingham Womencare Shelter to receive the set.

Once again, Builder Boards had taken on a life of its own—limited only by the imaginations of young people.

*8th grade students constructing Builder Boards can't resist testing them.*

# THE CEDAR PLAYHOUSE

*Cedar fence boards have the log-cabin look.*

## MATERIALS

- Approximately 300 linear feet of cedar 1" X 6".

  The basic house shown on the cover requires:

  | | |
  |---|---|
  | 36 6 1/2" connector pcs | = 20 lf |
  | 26 16" short wall pcs | = 36 lf |
  | 22 48" long wall pcs | = 88 lf |
  | 12 48" roof boards | = 48 lf |
  | gable-end assembly | = 12 lf |
  | total | = 204 lf |

  I would recommend buying 300 lf, which will allow plenty for working around the big knots, for mistakes, and for extra pieces that the kids will use as their structures become more elaborate.

- 400 2 1/2" sheet rock screws.  For reinforcing the corners.  More if you make a lot of extra pieces.
- Hook and loop fastener:   128" X 2" wide hooks; 144" X 2" wide loops
- One tube Sikaflex™ caulking for gluing hook and loop fastener to gable-ends and roof boards.
- 21' 6" of 3/4" (-) round to make the top of gable ends wider for 2" hook and loop fastener
- Approximately 20' 1" X 4" (left over fence boards) for box sides
- Masonite, or equivalent, for box bottoms, 1 pc 12 3/4" X 14", 3 pcs 12 1/2" X 16 3/8"

## TOOLS

- Staple gun with 3/8" staples
- Power planer for planing boards
- Table saw
- Hand saw
- Router with 1/4" corner round bit
- Vibrator sander

- Drill and bits
- Dust mask, ear protection, safety glasses
- Brace with screwdriver bit or power screwdriver
- Tape measure
- Square

## WOOD SELECTION

Fence boards are sometimes of poor quality, so you must pick through the pile at your lumberyard to find that one board in five or six good enough to use. Don't be in a hurry. Some lumberyards allow you to sort through the stock as long as you restack the pile carefully. At other yards, I find it helps to tell them what you are building (show them the plans) and ask for permission or offer to pay a little more to sort through the pile. You will have the best luck if you talk to them when they are not busy.

Reject boards that are warped, have long splits, large knots or rot. The thickness may vary widely; so reject very thin boards. You can make cardboard or scrap wood patterns of each of the three wall pieces and take them with you in order to make sure defects will not fall on the notches. I usually had to purchase five-or six-foot-long boards to find a good four-foot length for the long wall and roof pieces. The leftover pieces could often be made into smaller 6 1/2" or 16" pieces.

*The disassembled playhouse can be stored in the bottom of a closet.*

# CONSTRUCTION NOTES

- **Plane the boards to thickness.** The boards must be exactly the same thickness so that the notches of one board will fit over and into the notches of all the other boards. I planed mine to 11/16" and cut 3/4" notches.

- **Make the boxes** to hold two- and four-notch pieces. Make one box 12 3/4" X 14" with 1" X 4" sides for the two-notch pieces. Make 3 boxes 12 1/2" X 16 3/8" for the four- notch pieces.

- **Cut to length.** If the boards are different lengths, the notches will not match when stacking and therefore won't fit. A radial arm saw or chop saw makes this step easier, but you can cut them carefully by hand like I did.

## WALL PIECES

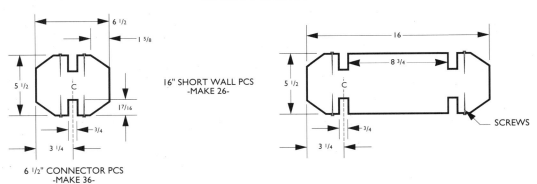

6 1/2" CONNECTOR PCS
-MAKE 36-

16" SHORT WALL PCS
-MAKE 26-

SCREWS

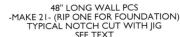

48" LONG WALL PCS
-MAKE 21- (RIP ONE FOR FOUNDATION)
TYPICAL NOTCH CUT WITH JIG
SEE TEXT

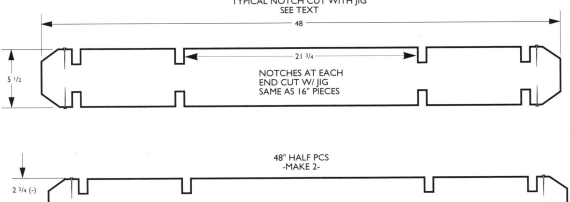

NOTCHES AT EACH
END CUT W/ JIG
SAME AS 16" PIECES

48" HALF PCS
-MAKE 2-

(1) FULL 48" PIECE RIPPED LENGTHWISE GIVES (2) PCS.

- **Accurately cut notches.** All the notches must be exactly the same width (board thickness plus 1/16"), the same depth (1 7/16" for 5 1/2" wide boards), and the same distance from the end of each board. If the notches are too wide or too deep, the pieces will fit together easily, but the resulting structure will be wobbly. If the interlocking notches are too snug, kids will have a difficult time putting them together and quickly will become frustrated. The boards should initially fit together quite snugly. After the edges of the notches are rounded with a router (1/4" round), the fit will loosen up a bit and, if necessary, you can loosen them a bit more with a few strokes of a rasp for the final fit. Better too loose than too tight.

Most people who have built things before and have power tools will figure out their own best method for cutting the notches quickly and accurately. For those who do not have much experience nor many power tools, the following is a description and diagram of a miter box jig I used to accurately cut all the notches by hand. See the jig drawings below. The dimensions given are for boards 5 1/2" wide and 11/16" thick. If you use wider or different thickness boards, you must refigure the jig dimensions.

## MITER BOX JIG

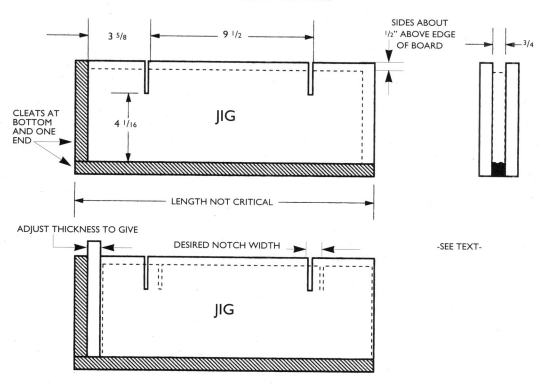

- **Using the jig.** Put the removable stick in the end of the miter box as shown below. Push a planed, cut-to-length board into the box. The board must fit tightly against both the end and the bottom of the jig. Put a clamp across the jig between the saw cuts to hold everything tight. Use a back saw to make the two cuts. Remove the stick, push the board tight up against the end of the miter box, clamp, and make two more cuts. This gives you a board like the one in #2 (opposite page). Now flip the board over (not end for end) and repeat the above procedure. Remove the board from the jig and knock out the pieces between the two saw cuts with a chisel so you have a board like that in #4.

  After cutting two boards using the above procedure, you can check the accuracy of the jig by fitting them together, notch to notch. This should be a snug fit. It will loosen up after you round the corners with a router. Check the fit of each board after it is made. This way creeping inaccuracies can be corrected right away. If the fit is too loose, the removable stick is too thick. Plane it down a hair and try again. If the fit is too tight, the stick is too thin. Make another a little thicker.

## USING THE JIG

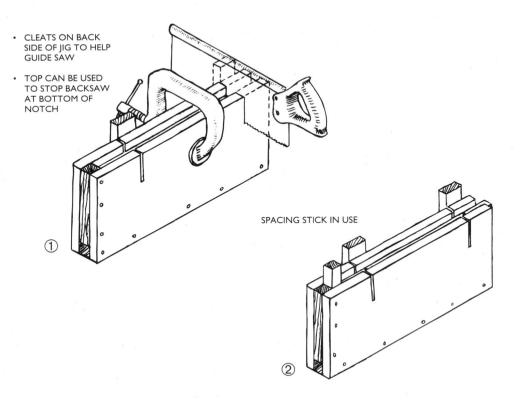

- CLEATS ON BACK SIDE OF JIG TO HELP GUIDE SAW

- TOP CAN BE USED TO STOP BACKSAW AT BOTTOM OF NOTCH

① 

SPACING STICK IN USE

②

## STEPS FOR EACH BOARD

1. MAKE JIG TO DIMENSIONS GIVEN.
   CUT ONE SIDE OF NOTCHES IN BOARD.

2. USE SPACING STICK TO CUT OTHER SIDE
   OF NOTCHES.
   - SEE TEXT -

3. TURN OVER IN JIG (NOT END FOR END)
   AND CUT SIDES OF NOTCHES IN OTHER
   EDGE.

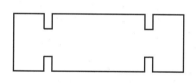

4. USE CHISEL TO CUT OUT NOTCHES
   - CLEAN UP BOTTOM OF NOTCHES -

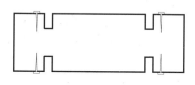

5. DRILL FOR AND INSTALL SCREWS TO KEEP
   ENDS FROM SPLITTING.

6. CUT OFF CORNERS.

7. USE 1/4" QUARTER ROUND ROUTER BIT TO
   RADIUS ALL EDGES AND CORNERS.

## GABLE ENDS

GABLE END
RAFTERS
-MAKE 2-

32

2 1/2

26°

CUT NOTCH AFTER ASSEMBLY

1/2" CUTAWAY OUTBOARD OF NOTCH

GABLE TOP PCS.
-MAKE 2-

5 1/2

C

11 5/16

GABLE BOTTOM PCS.
-MAKE 2-

NOTE: CAN BE CUT
FROM 48" WALL PIECE

22 5/8

C

NOTCH SPACING
TO MATCH 48"
WALL PCS.

5 1/2

1"

40 3/8

## GABLE END ASSEMBLY

2" HOOK LOOP
FASTENER

5/8" CORNER
ROUND

11/16" CEDAR
GABLE END
PIECE

1 GABLE END SECTION

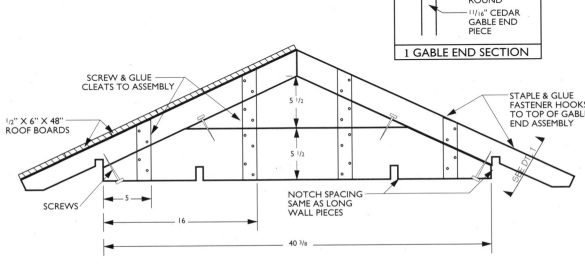

SCREW & GLUE
CLEATS TO ASSEMBLY

STAPLE & GLUE
FASTENER HOOKS
TO TOP OF GABLE
END ASSEMBLY

5 1/2

1/2" X 6" X 48"
ROOF BOARDS

5 1/2

SEE DT. 1

SCREWS

NOTCH SPACING
SAME AS LONG
WALL PIECES

5

16

40 3/8

- **Trim ends off and rout** with a 1/4" corner round. Cut the corners off each wall piece (1 5/8" back from the corner) as shown on page 12. Then rout with a 1/4" corner round bit around all the edges of each board. This makes the boards look nicer and allows them to slide together more easily.

- **Put the sheet rock screws into the ends of each notched board**, outboard of the notch, to keep the ends from splitting. Drill pilot holes first. See drawing of wall pieces page 12.

- **Make the gable-end assembly** as shown on the opposite page.

- **Plane the roof boards 1/2" thick.** Cut to dimensions given below. This way they are lighter and easier for the kids to handle. Round the corners and sand.

- **Glue and nail 5/8" corner round** to both sides of the top of the gable end pieces.

- **Glue and staple hook fastener** along the top of each gable-end assembly. Glue and staple loops to the bottom of each roof board. See inset page 16 and drawing below.

## ROOF BOARDS

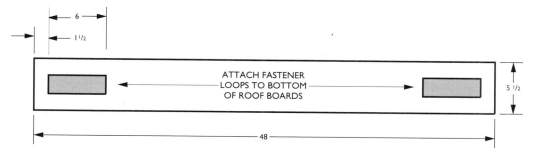

# PLYWOOD BUILDER BOARDS

*Builder Boards constructed from plywood allow more building options and are practically indestructible.*

## MATERIALS

- Four sheets $3/4$" birch or maple plywood - good both sides
- One sheet $1/2$" birch or maple plywood - good both sides
- Approximately one gallon water-based finish or equivalent
- Paint brush
- About sixty feet of $1/4$" nylon rope, shock cord or an old inner tube, to cut up for ties to hold the six-, eight-, and ten-notch pieces together
- Piece of aluminum for pattern: 5 $1/2$" X 48" X $3/16$"
- 30' of 1" X 4":  fir, pine, or cedar to make four boxes for carrying the two- and four-notch pieces
- Masonite, four pieces: 12 $3/4$" X 18 $3/4$"
- Thirty two 1 $5/8$" sheet rock screws for box corners
- Hook and loop fastener:
  Hooks: 66" X 2" for top of gable ends
  66" X $3/4$" for top of short roof support
  Loops:  18' X 2" for bottom of roof boards
- One tube Sikaflex™ caulking to glue hook and loop fastener to top of gable-ends and bottom of roof boards
- 11' of $5/8$" corner round, to make top of gable end wider for 2" hook and loop fastener
- Fiber-glass automobile body filler for filling voids in the plywood

# TOOLS

- Table saw
- Hand saw
- Hand vibrator sander
- Router
- Laminate trimming bit (bearing on the bottom)
- 1/4" (or 3/16") round router bit
- Staple gun and 3/8" staples, to staple hook and loop fastener

- Tape measure
- Safety goggles, ear protection, dust mask
- Square
- Hacksaw and file for making aluminum pattern
- Power screwdriver
- Caulking gun

# PLYWOOD SELECTION

I used 3/4" birch (good both sides) for the wall pieces and gable-ends and 1/2" birch (good both sides) for the roof.  Exterior fir plywood would be a better choice if Builder Boards are to be used outside extensively, but doesn't finish up as well.  Whichever you choose, remember 3/4" plywood is not always 3/4" thick.  Mine was 3/4" minus 1/32"; so I made the notches 13/16" wide, giving 1/16" plus 1/32" (3/32") for clearance.  Measure the plywood thickness before you make the pattern.  Make sure all the sheets are the same thickness and adjust the notch width if your plywood is thinner than 11/16".

The notch width is critical.  If the notches are too wide or too deep, the pieces will fit together easily, but the resulting structure will be wobbly.  If the interlocking notches are too snug, kids will become quickly frustrated.  The notch width should be between 1/16" and 3/32" greater than the plywood thickness.  One piece of plywood I bought was just a little thicker than the rest.  Since I didn't notice this until after the notches on two sheets had been cut, I had to go back and take a few strokes with a rasp to widen each of the notches I had already cut.

# CONSTRUCTION NOTES

- **Make boxes** for the two-and four-notch pieces: inside dimensions = 11 1/4" X 17 1/4", sides from 1" X 4", and bottom from Masonite or scrap paneling.  Make four boxes.

- **Cut the plywood,** except the gable-end pieces, into strips 5 1/2" wide.  Cut it into shorter lengths first to make it easier to handle.  See plywood layout drawings next page.   Using a thin saw blade, the kerf will be about 1/8", making the last piece about 3" wide.  Cut it down to 2 3/4", and use this last piece for the split pieces.

# PLYWOOD LAYOUT

### SHEET ONE: 3/4" BIRCH OR MAPLE

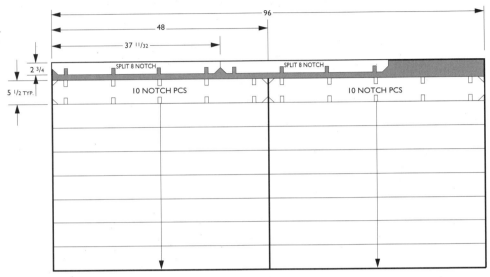

SHADED AREAS = SCRAP

# PLYWOOD LAYOUT

### SHEET TWO: 3/4" BIRCH OR MAPLE

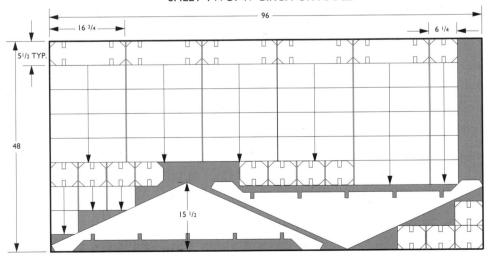

SHADED AREAS = SCRAP

# PLYWOOD LAYOUT
## SHEET THREE: 3/4" BIRCH OR MAPLE

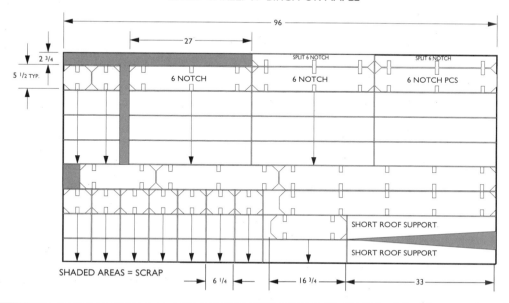

SHADED AREAS = SCRAP

# PLYWOOD LAYOUT
## SHEET FOUR: 3/4" BIRCH OR MAPLE

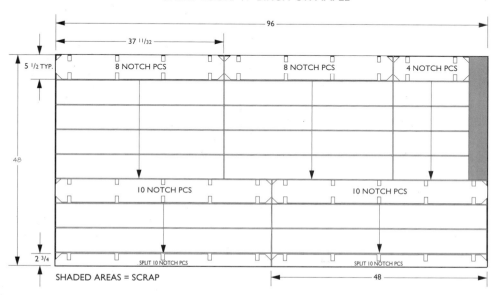

SHADED AREAS = SCRAP

## PATTERN-NOTCH LAYOUT

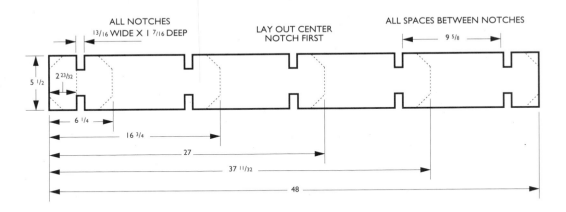

ALL NOTCHES
13/16 WIDE X 1 7/16 DEEP

LAY OUT CENTER
NOTCH FIRST

ALL SPACES BETWEEN NOTCHES

9 5/8

5 1/2

2 23/32

6 1/4

16 3/4

27

37 11/32

48

• **Make the pattern.** The notches must be cut accurately so that the notches of one board will match the notches of every other board. Making the smaller cedar set by hand is not so bad as most people suppose, but for the larger plywood version you will probably want to set up some method to cut the notches with power tools. I used a router with a laminate trimming bit (bearing on the bottom) to trace a pattern the exact shape of the notched boards. I first tried a plywood pattern. That was a mistake. With each pass, the bearing on the bottom of the router bit dug deeper and deeper into the soft plywood pattern, making each piece a hair wider than the last. By the time I got halfway through the house, the notches were very sloppy. I switched to an aluminum pattern to ensure it would not wear noticeably with each successive pass of the router.

Except for leaving the corners on, make the pattern from the dimensions of a finished ten-notch wall piece. Later, you will screw through these corners to hold the plywood strips in place under the pattern. Lay out the center notch first, using it as the base for the right and left notches. There is less error this way than if you start at one end and measure each notch from the one before. Another option is to have the pattern made by a steel fabrication company that has a computer controlled laser cutter. These machines are incredibly accurate and relatively inexpensive for "one off" production. The pattern could be made from steel, instead of aluminum, for additional savings.

## USING A ROUTER AND PATTERN TO CUT NOTCHES

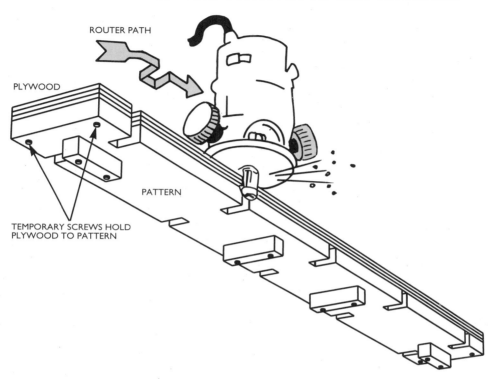

ROUTER PATH

PLYWOOD

PATTERN

TEMPORARY SCREWS HOLD
PLYWOOD TO PATTERN

- **Using the pattern:** Once the pattern is accurately made, turn it upside down and place a plywood strip (or strips) underneath each notch. This could be a single 48" piece, five two-notch pieces or any combination of pieces. Fasten the pattern and plywood strip(s) together by drilling holes in the pattern corners and putting screws through these holes into the corners (later to be cut off) of the plywood strip(s). Run the router with laminate trimming bit around the pattern. The bearing on the bottom of the bit traces the pattern while the cutter cuts the plywood strip in exactly the same shape as the pattern. Make a few pieces and check to be sure they fit together and come apart easily. If not, take a little more off your pattern notches. The fit is critical. If too snug, the kids become quickly frustrated and will not use the set. If too loose, the house will be wobbly.

  Be sure to clean the sawdust out of the pattern notches after each router pass. At first I didn't, and my plywood pieces kept coming out smaller than the pattern notches.

  Once the pattern is accurately made, you can build the basic house and add more pieces later. If this is a group project, you can pass the pattern around and have each person make a few pieces.

## GABLE ENDS

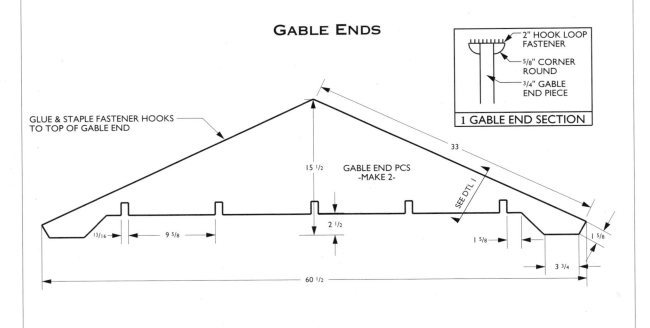

GLUE & STAPLE FASTENER HOOKS
TO TOP OF GABLE END

2" HOOK LOOP FASTENER

5/8" CORNER ROUND

3/4" GABLE END PIECE

**1 GABLE END SECTION**

15 1/2

GABLE END PCS
-MAKE 2-

33

SEE DTL I

2 1/2

13/16

9 5/8

1 5/8

1 5/8

3 3/4

60 1/2

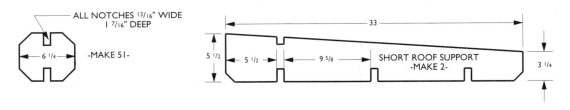

ALL NOTCHES 13/16" WIDE
1 7/16" DEEP

6 1/4

-MAKE 51-

33

5 1/2

5 1/2

9 5/8

SHORT ROOF SUPPORT
-MAKE 2-

3 1/4

- **Trim the corners.** After the notches have been cut, trim the corners off each plywood wall piece as shown in the pattern notch layout page 22.

- **Make the gable ends** and short roof pieces to the dimensions given above.

- **Glue (with Sikaflex™) and staple hook and loop fastener** hooks along the top of each gable-end assembly.

- **Round the corners** of all the pieces with a router and 1/4" corner round bit. Sand to remove rough spots and splinters.

- **Fill voids** in plywood with automobile body filler.

# PLYWOOD LAYOUT: ROOF BOARDS
### SHEET FIVE: 1/2" BIRCH

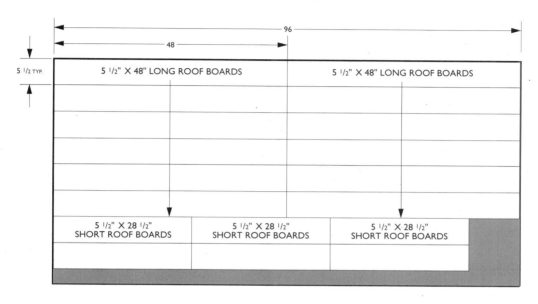

- **Cut the roof pieces** as shown above in sheet #5 plywood layout drawing. Round corners and sand. Glue and staple 6" strips of loops to the bottom of each roof board as shown below.

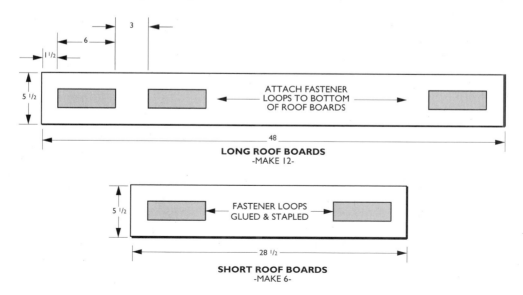

# SPLIT PIECES
### MAKE 2 OF EACH

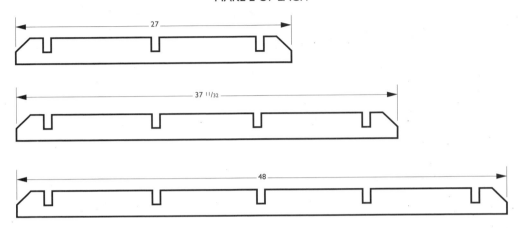

**Split Pieces** fit opposite each other in the first row of a structure to make the base flush with the ground.

- **Make the three-, four- and five-notch split pieces (above).** When assembling a structure, the split pieces fit in the first tier of a structure filling the half board gap, next to the floor, on opposite walls.

- **Finish all wood pieces** with at least two coats of water-based exterior varnish.

- **Make ties.** You will need some method of holding the long pieces together for storage and transport. Shock cord loops, circles cut from an inner tube or rope all work well. Teach the kids to stack the six-, eight-, and ten-notch boards in easy-to-carry piles and tie them through the notches at each end.

*Completed set of Builder Boards using five sheets of plywood.*

This last step completes the set. If this set is for your own children, quite possibly they have been unable to resist the temptation to experiment with unfinished pieces. If so, they may have a good idea about how to use Builder Boards before you've finished making all the pieces. If the set is for a daycare, church or school, you'll want to read the next chapter on how to present it to different ages or groups of children.

# WORKING WITH CHILDREN

## SUPERVISION

Builder Boards create problems for children to solve. They have to think ahead and work together. Initially, some of these problems can be frustrating so children need help, guidance and close supervision until they learn to use Builder Boards carefully.

Words often seem ineffective when working with groups of unfamiliar children. You can say, "Please don't walk on the boards," or "Lift straight up not at an angle," and they seem not to hear. Giving long explanations or repeating directions two or three times only results in frustration for you while the kids repeat the same errors. Demonstrate, and they see right away. I try to phrase my expectations in a non-threatening manner, something like, "I'm afraid someone is going to get hurt if you walk on boards. Let's stack them up."

*Initially children need guidance and supervision as they learn to use Builder Boards.*

It is common for enthusiastic adult helpers to offer too much advice, or offer it too early. Children learn and remember more when they solve problems for themselves.

I have developed some ground rules for use with children of different ages. It works best to allow preschoolers to become adept with the two-, four- and six-notch pieces before bringing out the whole set. Once they are comfortable with the shorter pieces, show them the eight- and ten-notch pieces and help them with the gable ends and roof.

Early elementary age children may want to figure things out for themselves. Show them how to lift from the center of a board to keep the corners from binding and caution them not to walk on boards. Careful observation will give you a sense of whether they need additional hints or would rather puzzle it out themselves. When it comes time to take a structure apart, demonstrate how to stack the longer boards in piles and put the two- and four-notch pieces in their boxes.

*Have children carry longer boards by holding them vertically.*

# AVOIDING CHAOS

With a classroom or a large group, a few guidelines and a demonstration go a long way toward a positive experience for all:

- Set a limit of four or five children at a time for work on the main structure. Six or eight working on the same project will certainly be chaotic and may result in hurt feelings. Others can work on an outbuilding such as a carport, fence or doghouse.

- Make a rule: "One board at a time." Have children hold the longer boards vertically in front of their bodies while carrying them. When children carry the longer boards horizontally, they bump into each other and everything else. For some reason, kids love to carry boards on their heads. This is not a good idea!

- Suggest trying to visualize the whole structure. Remind them to add boards to the low sides. Adjacent walls are best built up alternately so they interlock and support each other at the corners.

*One child on each end of roof board.*

- Assembly of the roof is probably the most complicated. Younger kids will need help handling the heavy gable ends and reaching the higher roof boards. Put one child on each end of a roof board. Working together, they can position a board they can't manage alone. Other times it works better to have one child inside the house carefully positioning boards delivered by other children. Regardless of whether assembling or disassembling, older children often need reminders to slow down and periodic demonstrations on how to carefully carry and position one board at a time. The roof (and most structures) are best disassembled from outside the structure, one board at a time.

- When disassembling, remove wall boards by holding them parallel to the floor. Kids tend to remove boards (especially the long ones) at an angle, causing the lower notch to bind. The harder they pull, the tighter the pieces are locked together. The solution is to put the board back where it was and lift it up parallel to the floor.

- Stop and stack. Unless instructed otherwise, children invariably take a structure apart as fast as they can, piling boards in a jumble around the base. Insist they slow down, take one long board off at a time, and stack it before removing another. Have them place the small pieces in their boxes as they work. When youngsters begin walking on boards, it is time to stop and stack.

  These ground rules may seem complicated but children pick them up quickly. Once you've walked them through a construction project or two, they will become competent and careful builders capable of teaching their friends and classmates to use Builder Boards.

# EXPERIENCED BUILDERS

Once children have mastered Builder Board basics, they begin to visualize different structures and talk about what they want to build. This provides an opportunity for them to work on a different level, to discuss and agree on a design. I witnessed an example of this process at a summer camp for students with disabilities.

A high school student (I'll call George) with Down's syndrome was working with a middle school student (I'll call Randy) who had difficulty speaking and using one arm. George was extremely good natured. Randy was a little contrary.

George had a very definite plan in mind and was proceeding to build it. Randy's plan was more nebulous. One of them would add a piece or two of which the other did not approve. There would be a long, mostly good natured discussion, and pieces might or might not be moved. And so it went. A few pieces added, big discussion, pieces added or subtracted or moved, and another big discussion. After nearly an hour of building, discussion and rebuilding, without adult interference, their creation was completed. They were obviously pleased both with their structure and with themselves for having created it together.

On another occasion, my son Andrew set out to build something with his friend Edward. They started with enthusiasm but no planning. Soon, with the walls halfway up, they realized it wasn't what they wanted. After considerable debate, they tore the half-built structure down and started over. With an agreed upon scheme, they went on to finish a tall house with a low flat-roof outbuilding.

*A more complicated structure.*

# POPULAR PROPS

Along with discussion and debate, which seem to occur naturally with Builder Boards, children love to include the use of props. Furniture is popular. Tables are built from stacked four-notched pieces covered with upside down two-and four-notch storage boxes.

I teach a shop class for children with woodworking and science projects, and kids often incorporate class projects into structures they've built. A stool built in class is a favorite place to sit inside a playhouse. An old garden hose, with cones taped to both ends, provides a telephone. A bank of solar cells with lights, bells, a fan and supporting wiring provide interior lighting, a doorbell and air conditioning. Thus children combine lessons in electricity and how sound travels with what they are learning about building and working with others.

Other props I've seen children use include flower boxes, curtains made from fabric scraps, a TV antenna fabricated from a coat hanger and a chimney built from a cardboard box.

# IN THE CLASSROOM

Over the years teachers have borrowed or built Builder Boards for their classrooms. They have been incorporated when children study shelter or early American pioneers. Small groups of students take turns building and rebuilding different structures in the back of the room. Kids often build a playhouse where they retreat to read, an island of privacy in a crowded classroom. Several teachers have reported students who did not do well with academics, but excelled at building or helping others build.

*A small retreat from the crowd.*

# COMMUNITY BUILDING

Community organizations that might use Builder Boards include schools, day-care centers and churches, anywhere there are young children. Since constructing a set of Builder Boards requires a significant investment of time and money, it is only logical to consider a community building project.

In my own community a church built a set for their day-care center. One church member was so intrigued by seeing a set of Builder Boards she not only bought the building plans, she bought the plywood too! Two builders from the church cut out all the pieces and other members did the sanding and finishing.

My own experience involved setting up eighth graders to construct a set of Builder Boards as part of a service learning project. This chapter documents that project and is to be used in conjunction with the measurements and construction details of Chapter Two.

# SERVICE LEARNING

Service learning is an integration of community service into student instruction and learning; it has become a part of many schools' curriculum. Some objectives of service learning projects are to:
• meet real community needs
• provide a collaboration between school and community
• allow time for students to think, talk and write about their project
• expand student learning beyond the classroom
• help foster a caring for others

Students might work in a nursing home, at a food bank, animal shelter or on an environmental restoration project. At Whatcom Middle School in Bellingham, Washington, where this project took place, eighth graders were required to choose a service project and work on it one morning a week for ten weeks. Writing assignments in the form of journals, with reflections about their project, were incorporated into regular classroom assignments. Nine students chose constructing a set of Builders Boards and giving it to a community organization as their project.

A college student volunteer helped the eighth graders through the process of giving the Builder Boards away. Students talked about who might benefit from receiving Builder Boards and brainstormed questions to ask potential recipients. Two students designed a questionnaire to screen interested agencies. Using a phone script, they called over fifty possible agencies and individuals, and then presented their findings to the rest of the group.

After construction was almost completed, we took a portion of one day to discuss and decide who was to receive the Builder Boards. Aside from helping with questions like, "What is a non-profit organization?" and whether or not to give it to a religious organization, adult helpers stayed out of the way. Taking the process very seriously and after lengthy discussion they unanimously chose Bellingham's Womencare Shelter as the recipient. The Shelter provides refuge for women and children who are victims of domestic violence.

After the project was finished, five of the students delivered Builder Boards to the Womencare Shelter business office and built a playhouse for an enthusiastic staff. For security reasons they were unable to deliver it to the actual shelter and see the children use it. This was a disappointment but part of the lesson.

# ORGANIZING A STUDENT FRIENDLY PROJECT

When I conceived this project, I wanted to demonstrate that inexperienced students could complete a sophisticated project using hand tools. Hand tools are safe, quiet and surprisingly efficient. I felt they would complement eighth graders' need to expend energy, socialize, work and play all at the same time. Further, I believe that once you become competent with hand tools and the nature of the tasks involved in using them, then and only then can you make reasonable choices about the use of power tools. In the interests of efficiency for a very routine task, we used power sanders, which are relatively safe.

My first step was to work out construction details. For each step that required repeated, exacting measurements, I designed a jig. After working out details of each step and building the jigs I felt confident the carpentry would move smoothly.

Building the playhouse with a group was a real organizational problem. There were about fifteen different jobs to do, some challenging, some repetitive. There was an order and sequence to the jobs although, within that sequence, there was some flexibility. Availability of jigs and choice of tools also determined organizational options. The challenge was to intersperse the tedious tasks like edge rounding and sanding with the more interesting ones, match the kids' interest and abilities to the tasks, and to switch jobs frequently enough to sustain interest and enthusiasm.

*Using a sunform plane to round corners.*

## JOBS LIST

1. Cut pieces to length
2. Cutting the corners
3. Rounding edges
4. Sanding edges
5. Cutting the notches down
6. Forming notches by removing plywood between saw cuts
7. Check fit and quality control
8. Oil finish
9. Laying out and cutting gable ends
10. Wood burning gable end(s)
11. Gluing and stapling hook and loop fastener to top of gable end and bottom of the roof boards
12. Building boxes to hold two- and four-notch pieces
13. Cut, round, sand, and oil roof boards
14. Make ties for roof boards and six- and ten-notch pieces
15. Questionnaire and phone calls

Although I did not institute it the first day, it soon became obvious a schedule was necessary. On the first day the kids expected a break every time the bell rang and the rest of the school moved from class to class. A five minute break every 40 minutes upset our rhythm so, on the second day, I proposed the following schedule:

## THE SCHEDULE:

| | |
|---|---|
| 8:30-8:45 | Discussion of jobs to be done |
| | Safety, new tools |
| 8:45-9:15 | First Job |
| 9:15-9:45 | Second job |
| 9:45-10:00 | Break (with donuts) |
| 10:00-10:15 | Questions, problems, review, discussion |
| 10:15-10:45 | Third Job |
| 10:45-10:55 | Clean up |

This schedule worked well although, once it was established, we didn't always feel the necessity to stick with it. The break in the middle was crucial, and the donuts became a revered ritual. If a student had started a job, such as building a box, they often went on to finish it. Because there was a tendency to gravitate toward the more interesting jobs and away from tedious rounding and sanding, the problem was to be sure each student got her chance at the fun jobs and did his share of the repetitive ones. If a youngster was doing a job no one else wanted to do and they wanted to keep doing it, I saw no reason to switch. After discussing the fairness issue, I left it mostly up to them. A future tactic might be to have everyone round corners and/or sand for the first 20 or 30 minutes.

# CONSTRUCTION DETAILS: NOTCHED PIECES

For each notched piece there were eight steps. On the first day I talked about safety, introduced four of the eight steps, and we went to work.

- **Cut to length.** I had cut four plywood sheets into strips (see Chapter 2, pages 20 and 21) so the kids started with a pile of strips 5 1/2" wide and 48" long. These strips had to be cut into the correct number of proper length pieces. The long strips were inserted into the jig (below) and a cut made at the proper slot. This operation was repeated until we had 43 two-notch pieces, 27 four-notch pieces and 10 six-notch pieces. I had precut the long roof boards and the 10-notch pieces to length.

  This jig worked well. The students' tendency was to get in a hurry and to be swept up by the cutting, so I monitored to make sure they cut the proper number of each length piece. Working in pairs helped, one sawing while the other set up the next piece. Some workers were so diligent they developed blisters. I encouraged them to slow down and pace themselves. With one hundred 5 1/2" cuts, pacing is important!

## CUT TO LENGTH JIG

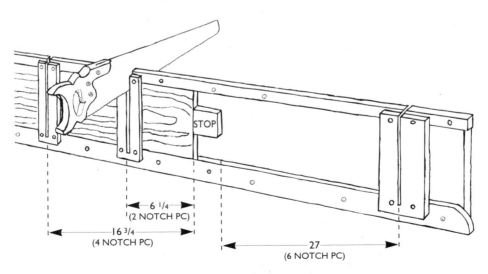

6 1/4 (2 NOTCH PC)

16 3/4 (4 NOTCH PC)

27 (6 NOTCH PC)

## CORNER JIG

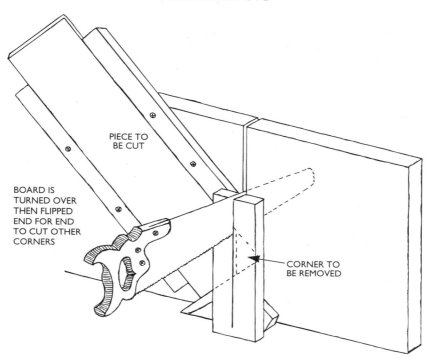

PIECE TO
BE CUT

BOARD IS
TURNED OVER
THEN FLIPPED
END FOR END
TO CUT OTHER
CORNERS

CORNER TO
BE REMOVED

- **Cutting the corners off:** See jig above. This was straightforward and difficult to make a mistake, but it was hard work. We made almost 100 notched wall pieces and each piece had four corners to be removed. Often, after 10 minutes (two or three boards), they needed a rest.

- **Rounding the edges:** There were over 1000 feet of edges to be rounded. Each piece, including the gable ends and roof boards, had to be rounded. Rounding the edges makes the pieces safer, easier to handle and gives a more attractive finish, but it is a tedious job. We started rounding edges on the first day, and finished on the eighth.

  I started by giving a lesson on how to use a plane, explaining how sharp (very) they are. Using a plane is a skill developed from practice. I demonstrated, let them practice on the actual boards, observed them, showed them again and let them practice as many times as needed. Spoke shaves and surforms became the tools of choice for the ends and short pieces while corner planes and block planes were used for the longer six-and ten-notch pieces and the roof boards. We rounded all the edges of each board before we cut the notches in it.

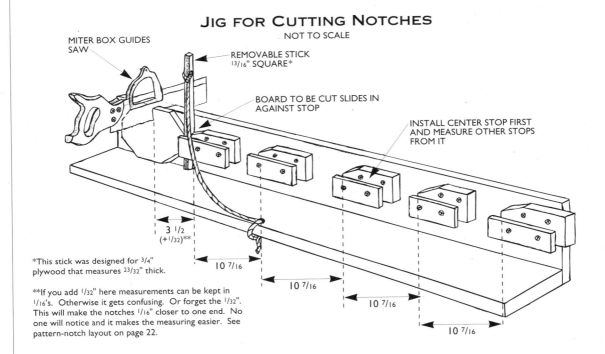

## JIG FOR CUTTING NOTCHES
### NOT TO SCALE

MITER BOX GUIDES
SAW

REMOVABLE STICK
13/16" SQUARE*

BOARD TO BE CUT SLIDES IN
AGAINST STOP

INSTALL CENTER STOP FIRST
AND MEASURE OTHER STOPS
FROM IT

3 1/2
(+1/32)**

10 7/16

10 7/16

10 7/16

10 7/16

*This stick was designed for 3/4"
plywood that measures 23/32" thick.

**If you add 1/32" here measurements can be kept in
1/16's. Otherwise it gets confusing. Or forget the 1/32".
This will make the notches 1/16" closer to one end. No
one will notice and it makes the measuring easier. See
pattern-notch layout on page 22.

- **Cutting the notches down.** The width, depth and the spacing of the notches is critical. If the notches are too wide, or deep, the house will be wobbly. If the notches are too tight, kids using the house will become quickly frustrated. If the spacing between the notches isn't exactly the same, the boards will not line up when the house is built.

    To keep all these cuts in the right place, I made a jig using a metal miter box to hold a back saw in exactly the right place. I used carefully measured stops to gauge the distance between notches and a stick that was 1/16" thicker than the notch width to gauge the notch width. Although there are several steps to using this jig, the kids caught on quickly and the notches came out in the right place.

    Use the jig as follows: Mark one end of the board being notched with a light pencil mark. This marked end will always fit against the jig stop no matter which notch is being cut. Install the proper stop on the jig. The first stop for cutting the first notch, the second stop for the second notch, etc. Push the board tight against the stop, clamp in place, and make the first cut. The miter box should be adjusted so the saw will only cut to and not beyond the proper notch depth (1 7/16"). Unclamp the board, flip it over (not end for end) and make the second cut. Next put the removable stick between the jig stop and the board. Push the board tight against the stick (and stop) and make the second cut in the top. Flip the board over again and make the second cut in the bottom of the board. Cut the first notch in a number of boards before switching to the next stop for the 2nd notch. Continue the same method for the 3rd, 4th, and 5th notches in the longer boards.

- **Sanding the edges.** The edges that had been rounded needed sanding. Another long job. We had a sanding table with a blower to suck saw dust away from the boards as we sanded. We used two orbital finishing sanders with 80 grit flooring sandpaper.

*At work on the sanding table.*

- **Form notch by removing plywood between saw cuts.** Use a coping saw to cut between the two saw cuts. The tendency was to clamp the longer boards in the vice up high so that they could cut two or three notches without moving the board in the vice. This did not work because the board moved back and forth instead of being cut. After a demonstration and some trial and error, most kids found it easiest to put the notch they were working on as close to the vice jaw as possible and move the board after cutting out opposite notches.

- **Check fit/quality control.** Because notch width, depth and spacing is so critical, it is necessary to check each and every notch. I stationed the jig for cutting notches next to the vice for removing the plywood between the saw cuts so the students doing these jobs could communicate with each other. If there was a problem, it could be corrected before many pieces were cut. I made it the responsibility of the person removing the plywood from the notch to ensure each notch was the proper width and depth and had the proper spacing.

- **Oil finish.** This was straightforward and the kids enjoyed doing it. We used 1 1/2 gallons of Watco clear oil, two coats on each piece, applying it with brushes and wiping with rags. Later, I switched to a water-based varnish instead of the oil finish. It is less toxic during application and has a harder finish.

# CONSTRUCTION DETAILS: FINISHING UP

- **Layout and cutout of the gable ends.** This was an exacting job for inexperienced woodworkers but they enjoyed the challenge. Two students worked together, and I walked them through it step by step. After cutting out and notching of the gable end, one student wrote in her journal, *"I learned it is very important to make accurate cuts."* Another wrote, *"Yesterday I learned how to cut the gable ends on the roof of the playhouse and it was a lot harder than I expected. I didn't measure some of the boards and I messed up and so I need to recheck my measurements before I cut the boards."*

- **Wood burning the gable end.** Burning the school's name, their individual names and a design into one gable end was a popular activity that could be expanded to include both sides of both gable ends.

- **Gluing and stapling hook and loop fastener** to the top of gable end and bottom of the roof boards.

- **Building the boxes** to hold the two- and four-notch pieces was a straightforward and popular project, although it requires accurate measurements. Usually two students worked together.

- **Cut, round, sand and oil the roof boards** using the same process as rounding and sanding of the notched pieces.

*Putting finish on Builder Boards.*

- **Cut and wash inner tube ties** for roof boards and the six- and ten-notch pieces

- **Questionnaire and phone calls.** On the third day it had become apparent that two of the students were not wildly enthusiastic about woodworking. They probably felt about woodworking like I feel about writing questionnaires and making phone calls, so when we asked for volunteers to write a questionnaire and make phone calls, we had two eager volunteers for an important job.

# A MAGICAL PROCESS

The last day was exciting. As some students finished the last pieces, the rest took the playhouse outside to be assembled for the first time. They built and rebuilt it several times, discussing shapes, entrances and the door and window placement. One student later wrote in his journal, *"I was amazed at what we created and are going to give to the lucky kids who are going to get it. Most of us want to keep it for ourselves."*

Here are other journal entries that illustrate how the students felt about this project:

*"The wood... would just be sitting there no matter if it just sat there for a minute or days. We changed that. We changed that wood into something uniquely made by us and extraordinarily beautiful."*

*"I thought this was going to be easy but it was really hard work."*

*"The unusual thing that happened was that everyone got along so well and there were no serious fights."*

*"..Now that we have worked for four weeks I think it is easier to be honest with him...I like that he is not a strictomaniac."*

*"All the hard work, the elbow grease, the toil, the donuts have finally paid off. It looks like we'll have the playhouse done on time."*

*"I think building a house would be an interesting project that I would like to try."*

*"When I got off the phone with Womencare, I almost cried. I told Carolee privately that those women over there, and their children are in a 'sad predicament' and she told me domestic violence is one of the less funded items in our community."*

*"I wish I could do this again with a group."*

A builder's parent said, *"This is the only thing in school he's interested in."*

There is something magical about the process of building, the transformation of raw materials by knowledge, skill and persistence into a beautiful and useful product. This is especially true of building for children. They are easy to please and appreciative of both the effort and the product. Watching teenagers capture some of this magic was rewarding. I have always felt building is an arena in which I have a tangible positive effect. I think our eighth grade builders felt the same way. In a world where things may seem incomprehensible or beyond control, here was real work where their efforts clearly made a difference.

Most of the kids who worked on this set of Builder Boards were sorry to see the project end. Several claimed they would have started the next day to build another. This work gave them the confidence to consider other projects. As one student said, *"Before this I had only built a couple things out of wood. Now that I have finished a project this big, I feel like I could go on and do something on my own..."*

Perhaps, when older, if they want to build their own cabin in the woods they won't be afraid to start. Or maybe they'll help build houses for Habitat for Humanity. Whatever the effect on their future, they can take satisfaction in the knowledge that, because of their efforts, children at the Womencare Shelter will be able to use their hands and imaginations to build the house they don't have.

*Satifaction in a completed project.*

# NOTES

# NOTES

# NOTES

# ABOUT THE AUTHOR

**Jack McKee** has worked as a mechanic, remodeled houses, built small boats, designed and constructed equipment for special needs children and cast bronze.

For the last ten years he has created equipment and taught classes for children integrating science, carpentry, and mechanics through the parks department, the public schools, and the Childlife Montessori School. His articles have appeared in *Home Education, Tech Directions, Early Childhood Today,* and *Wooden Boat.* He has taught bronze casting workshops and teaches "Woodworking with Kids," a workshop for teachers.

He lives in Bellingham, Washington with his wife, Candy Meacham. His two sons, Ben and Andrew, can usually be found sailing.

# ORDER FORM

Please send me _____copies of
**BUILDER BOARDS** by Jack McKee at $12.95 each.

*Add $2.00 Shipping and Handling*
*WA state residents add 7.8% tax*

Send payment to:

## HANDS ON BOOKS
1117 Lenora Court
Bellingham, WA 98225
(360) 671-9079

Your name _____

Address _____

City _____

State _____ Zip_____